MY DOG, MY CHILD
BLUE THE TERMITE SNIFFER DOG

OTHER BOOKS BY GLORIA BURLEY

Blood & Guts
Medical Mysteries - Digital Edition
Available through www.gloriaburley.com

©Gloria Burley

Published in Airlie Beach, QLD. 2016
ISBN-13: 978-1533434678
ISBN-10: 1533434670

MY DOG, MY CHILD

I look down at the orange/grey head at my feet. There really is nothing like the fidelity of a faithful dog. The love generated by this lovely soul. He doesn't ask for much apart from food and protection. In return he provides companionship bordering on love.

Blue came to us at the age of 12 months – a handsome tri-coloured dog. Orange head with matching ears. Dark orange eyes with dark patches around them like the most perfect make-up. The white muzzle goes up between the eyes and he has freckles on his nose. His body is white with a jacket of black rimmed with orange like his head. He has an unusual white pattern on his back that looks rather like the Nike tick with a few stars.

He is a beautiful dog.

Many childless couples console themselves with a dog. Little wonder really as a dog is a wonderful companion that can bring great joy, not to mention make you feel needed and wanted just like a child does. A child may run to the door when you come home and so does the dog. Eyes shining, ail wagging and you feel like a king or queen.

It is believed that dogs have a vocabulary of about 300 words, rather like a two year old child. Of course, they remain at this stage for ever which can be very endearing. There is no doubt that Blue can understand simple commands and there is also no doubt that he is a very independent little dog who will only do things if he feels like it or there is a food reward involved.

When given a double command like "stay here, sit down" either he gets confused and only does one of them or else he only does one of them to show that he is retaining his independence by not obeying completely.

Blue has no interest in toys which he may chew on for a few minutes before discarding them. We gave him a small lamb that we bought in a kid's toyshop and he slept with it in his kennel. Amazingly although he had small tugs of war with this lamb, he never ripped it apart as he has done with other toys. That is until another dog came into the house but more of that later.

Like a two year old child, Blue hates to be left alone. He becomes very destructive as if to punish us for leaving him. I was only exposed to the intelligence of a dog when Ivan decided he should get a termite sniffer dog to enhance his pest control business. He contacted a young guy who worked for a pest control company in Townsville and who had a lot of experience training bomb disposal dogs in the Army. Adam felt that he could train a dog to do almost anything and immediately set about looking for a suitable dog. He found a six month old beagle, a real Houdini who ran away so often that he spent most of his time on a chain in the backyard of his owners. Adam took him home to share his garden with four other dogs, all mutts. Blue stood out like a prince. The beagle was always digging his way out when Adam took his eyes off him. Of course he only told us this once he handed him over at the end of his training.

We chose the name Blue because it is only one syllable. I had friends who called their Alsatian dog Balthazar – what a mouthful to call when the dog runs away. Adam brought Blue to meet us towards the end of his six month training. Blue sat at Adam's feet most of the time, completely under his power. He was a very small, skinny dog. I was appalled to learn that Adam had forgotten to bring him some food and suggested we give him a bowl of cornflakes!

Ivan and Blue underwent a day of training together and Adam explained how important it was to make Blue feel that he was playing when he was searching for termites. All working dogs need a reward and it soon became apparent that the only reward Blue was interested in was food. Even though we provided him with various toys, Blue looked at them all with disdain but when the food came out, his pupils grew very big, the look of love.

Blue has not exactly been over-worked in Ivan's business. On average he goes termite sniffing once a week. He is not needed in new houses or where there are pets present as their smell will distract him.

As with any working dog, Blue needs to know when he was on duty and this means putting a harness on him and getting him excited about his job. Ivan leads him around the perimeter of the dwelling, all the time saying "seek it on" and when Blue's nose detects the presence of termites, he sits down. Ivan then says "show me" at which point, Blue points to the termites with his nose and then the inevitable reward, a handful of dog pellets. These basic commands and responses are taught to most working dogs.

A dog's nose is hundreds of times more sensitive than that of a human. They can even be trained to pick up the smell of cancer. The training involves exposing them to the substance that one wishes the dog to track and rewarding them when they signal it. They can also be trained to help people with PTSD, diabetes, or a disability where the person needs assistance. They can be trained to open doors by pulling on a cord, make phone calls by pushing a big button, bring medication or other things and cheer up depressed people by nudging or pawing them. Termite training takes about six months.

The rest of the time Blue is on Easy Street – he spends a lot of his time sleeping and has various areas around the garden where he tries to cool down. He loves to dig a spot out of the earth to find coolness underneath. In the house, he lies splayed out on his tummy with his legs along the ground ensuring that his body is in close contact with the coolness of the tiles. Not being a large dog, it is often difficult to see Blue when he lies down underneath shrubs or in long grass or when he finds a spot to lie underneath a table or behind a chair.

Unfortunately, Blue cannot be trusted to walk without a lead as he would escape at every opportunity. As a young dog, Blue would bolt as soon as he saw a chance which meant trying to hold him back when a door was opened. We tried a collar that would give him a quick shock if he ran off but he ran away so fast, he got out of range very quickly.

Blue could run as fast as a greyhound and disappear completely in double quick time, only returning several hours later when he felt like it. Like most hunting dogs Blue has been blessed with a lot of energy – they have been bred to locate and chase after game such as hares and they have to be prepared to run over all sorts of terrain for hours if necessary. Like Pointers, they stand stock still on three legs, tail straight out, nose pointing towards the prey but most of the time, Blue's nose is pointing towards the pantry or the refrigerator.

Once he disappeared for two whole days and we were sure that we had lost him as the area was known for wild dingoes who call to stray dogs, enticing them into the pack and then killing them for food.

After many disappearances and prodigal returns, we realized that Blue was not only an escape artist 'par excellence' but also that he could take care of himself. He sniffed at things very warily, always jumping back if he was unsure, rather like a cat. It was obvious that Blue was a big believer in the maxim 'he that fights and runs away, lives to fight another day' and we imagined that he fled at the first sign of any trouble with bigger dogs. He would return home from time to time with bite marks but nothing serious.

Once however, Blue came off second best when I took him for a walk on the lead along an unfamiliar street and he was set upon by a vicious dog. I was told that this dog had 'raped' a small dog in his street and had the run of the garden when his owner was at work, often bailing up other dogs. As the assailant clamped his teeth into Blue's neck, I screamed for help whilst trying to pull the dogs apart. Blue, in his excitement and fury, unwittingly bit my finger and he ended up with a deep gash in his neck which poured pus for a day or two. The perpetrator was the subject of a visit from a ranger and subsequently put down after other people complained about him.

On another occasion, Blue was the attacker when he was momentarily off the lead after a swim in the lake behind the house and a boxer dog crossed his path. The boxer was on a lead and his owner tried to hold him and once again Blue's sharp teeth left a lasting impression on the owner's arm which cost us time and money as we were petrified that we would have to put Blue down. The strange thing is that Blue had played with the boxer in their younger days. There were several other dogs in the area that became enemies as they grew into adults.

One morning I had just reached my neighbour Ilse's house when two tough looking bull terriers, fortunately on leads, came around the corner and we all came face to face. These dogs had always worried me and they were show dogs. Pride and joy of the family no doubt. I dived into Ilse's garden and Blue, no doubt sensing my distress, began to bark like mad which made the other two act viciously. So bad in fact that one dog turned on the other and chewed it to bits. The white dog was now red, bleeding profusely. Ilse grabbed a digeridoo and began to try to put it down the throat of the attacker. I just kept screaming until a male neighbor came to help separate them. He informed the young female owner that one dog would have to be put down and loaded the loser into the back of his truck whilst Ilse took charge of the winner – I must add that Ilse is 86 years old. She has no fear. I only ever see the white dog on walks and give him a wide berth.

A neighbor told me a horror story about a woman who had a small dog and she took it to a friend's house but as she was worried about their dog, she kept her dog on her lap. Eventually she succumbed to the reassurance of her friends and put her dog on the floor. It was immediately attacked and killed in front of her. She ended up in a psychiatric hospital. The same neighbor told me that if his Scottish terriers were ever attacked, he would kill the attacker. Parents say they would kill for their child.

Beagles are not normally vicious dogs. In fact, they are so gentle that they are chosen as dogs to use for drug and food sniffing in airports. Their size and 'teddy bear' looks make them ideal to use around people. Blue is intact, Ivan refusing to let his dog suffer the ignominy of a snip and the loss of his manhood.

ROMANTIC BLUE

Blue's first girlfriend was a little bitch and I do mean bitch. She lived a few doors away and came on heat for the first time when we had been living in our new house only a few weeks and we were waiting for the fence to be constructed. Blue was tied up to prevent any escapes. She approached him and before anyone knew what was happening, there was a full scale orgy going on in the back garden. I felt like a mother who was losing her son to another woman for the first time. I ran to tell the dog's owner what was happening but he just seemed amused and not in the least bit worried about the possibility of having several puppies in the not too distant future.

The bitch returned several times over the next year or so before the family moved away. Blue was then introduced to a male beagle called Buddy who was very different to Blue. He was heavier and darker with no white at all. There must have been some sense of recognition for one of his own because when the dog left, Blue threw his head back and howled like a wolf. The only time that he has done this. The other beagle seemed to titillate Blue whenever he came around and there have been some sexually embarrassing moments for Blue. He has no qualms about being labeled gay.

He was 8 when he had his first real affair. Neighbors had seen Blue around the traps and wanted him to mate with their 3 year old beagle. Blue apparently did a very good job, almost completely wearing himself out. In fact, for about ten days afterwards he became depressed and was not even keen to walk on the beach, something he always loved. He would not leave my side and did not even need to be on a lead which is a very rare and strange event.

At this time, it must be said that Ivan was in the USA and had left his truck at the repair shop. Blue often went into the garage and lay there and it is possible that as every sign of Ivan had been removed – his truck, his clothes, etc. Blue felt that Ivan had gone. It is hard to know what the real cause was but it was obvious to all that Blue was very depressed. I even took him to the vet who confirmed that physically there was nothing wrong with him.

For a while we had to lift him into the car as he was too weary to jump in where as a young dog he could jump from a standing pose about four foot into the air, if not higher. This is due to the fact that dogs have powerful hindquarters equipped for speed with large, long muscles. Energy is stored in the muscles and tendons and the flexed hind legs enable him to use them as springs to get him out of trouble quick smart. The fact that dogs have four legs means that the weight is spread with four points of hold and greater agility than we humans. The speed, power and fine sense of balance are similar to the cats of prey who still need all these things to trap and kill their food.

A DAY IN THE LIFE...

Blue starts his day very early. He opens his eyes at dawn and in summer this is very early. Since we have had Blue, I have to go to bed earlier than usual as I know that I will be up at first light. He signals his presence by scratching on the door which gets louder and louder until he is admitted into the house. Whilst I retreat back to my bed, Blue makes himself comfortable, supposedly on the floor but I have caught him napping on the sofa at various times. He at least had the grace to look guilty when he caught.

Blue is very keen to have his morning walk as early as possible. Dawn would suit him fine but he has to wait until I can wake up which takes anything from a few minutes to a few hours. I am never keen to meet anyone when I take Blue for his early morning walk. I can't bear the thought of trying to make polite conversation when I am so tired and barely awake. Blue, of course, is full of beans. I usually walk him on a lead but from time to time, when I am fed up of being dragged along the beach at breakneck speed, I let him run. He has learnt over the years to stick to the open spaces and whenever he heads for the bushes, he is called back. He comes back if he feels like it.

I cannot say the walk is a relaxing experience. My eyes are peeled for other dogs. Sometimes I have seen big dogs wandering around on their own, probably escapees. I was rushed one day by a cattle dog, one of a gang of three and I was petrified the other two were going to join him but I managed to pull Blue back into the garden as we were very close to home.

Blue has two homes – one in town where we spend Monday to Friday and one at the beach where we spend weekends. It is rare to meet anyone on the beach normally but there have been odd occasions when we have encountered other dogs, so I have to pick my times. Usually when no-one else wants to walk because it is too hot or it is too early. It is always worrying to see whether or not the dogs will just sniff each other and keep moving or whether there will be a big fight. I have noticed that dogs stop in their tracks when they meet and eye each other up for a while before lunging at one another. The lunge can end in hugs and kisses or in a full scale battle. Before every walk nowadays I send out a prayer that my walk will be peaceful and uneventful. I try very hard to remain calm so that my emotions do not travel down the leash to Blue. He picks up on this and gets as agitated as I do. Once I screamed as I raced him into the bushes away from two big dogs who were no on a lead. The owner took absolutely no notice but Blue silenced me by biting me on the leg. He knew he had to do something and that certainly shut me up – I was shocked that my own little dog would bite me!

The town house is situated near a lake so he has very pleasant walks, both enabling him to have a dip and cool off when the weather is hot as it often is in the tropics. Blue has endeared himself to an old Germany lady, Ilse, who has a small dog called Molly. When we walk together, the dogs are the best of friends – sniffing and scratching in unison.

Blue is not a very brave dog unlike the legendary grey wolf or *canis lupus* from which all dogs are descended and share 99.96 percent of their DNA. More than 30,000 years of domestication have produced a bond with man and dog that cannot be matched. Recent studies show that it is not necessary to dominate the dog as 'head of the pack' but rather treat them like a wayward child and give them love and attention.

When we first took Blue for a walk along the beach he was petrified by the sound of the waves breaking on the shore. Even a leaf falling from a tree could make him jump. He hates parties or to hear any loud noises. When he is afraid he hides under his master's bed whether or not the master is in it. When a cyclone threatens, he jumps in the car, only to emerge when the danger has passed. Blue sees the car as an extension of us and represents his territory and safety. There have been times when we have left him in the car whilst we take in a two hour show rather than leave him alone at home. He usually jumps straight into the driver's seat and goes to sleep.

Blue is a delicate soul. He enjoys sniffing flowers and eating blades of grass in a most delicate fashion. When the need to evacuate his bowels arises he usually leaves his calling card balanced on leaves or flowers like an offering. He backs up to the plant and balances on his four legs whilst gazing up at his walker. He then usually scratches the ground like a wild bull with a look of total pride on his face. He is very fit and agile and when he raises his leg to relieve himself, he lifts it so high that he appears to be over-balancing but, like a ballet dancer, he is in complete control. For a small dog, I am surprised at how much food comes out of him on a regular basis – sometimes three or four times a day.

Beagles were bred in England to run with the hounds and chase after hares. They are pack animals. Apparently they are the only dogs who have not quite bonded with humans completely and prefer the company of other dogs, or the pack. The tip of Blue's tail is white and when he runs into long grass, this is often the only part of him that can be seen and this was also part of the breeding process. His tail is a great indication of how he is feeling. Mostly he holds it straight up and of course wags it wildly when he is happy. The wagging can extend to his whole body when he is really happy. However, the tail droops when he is unhappy or being chastised. Fear can make his tail go so far down that it turns to touch his tummy.

Blue will eat anything. His favourite is a dead animal, usually a kangaroo, which has become dessicated by the sun and can be smelt long before it is seen. There have been times when he has attempted to drag a big kangaroo carcass back home. If he is lucky enough to find a bone or something similar, he makes every effort to take it home with him where he can eat it at his leisure. If it is really too big for him to carry, I try to show him that I am assisting him rather than trying to pinch his find. It takes him a while to realize that I am not going to keep his bone for myself.

Blue is a grazer, like me. He eats all day long – small amounts, perhaps a dog biscuit or a tiny piece of my food. When I walk outside with a plate full of food, he follows along closely, even preceding me in his mad rush to join me for a meal. His main meal consists of meat and dog biscuits. Ilse has given him lots of chicken, bacon, sausages, fish. He adores Ilse and she loves him. I try to give him more protein than carbohydrate and although Ivan accuses him of being fat (transference?),Blue presents as a slim well looked after dog and is often mistaken for a puppy – he has a nice waist.

He always stops at Ilse's gate and sniffs the air to see if she is there. Sometimes Ilse comes to the gate when we are the other side of the lake and if Blue sees her, I might as well let him go because he can run to her in a minute or two. I know he is safe to be running off the lead because he will not go past Ilse's house. He flies straight past Molly to Molly's bowl full of biscuits and other treats. He gobbles everything up while Ilse just laughs at 'the naughty little dog'.

When Blue takes off through a hole in the fence, I call Ilse first because her house will be his first port of call. She welcomes him with food and he is completely at home in her house, going through the drawers and cupboards looking for food.

If Blue comes across an old smelly carcass on the beach, he rolls himself in it with the greatest joy. This is to disguise his own smell so that he can approach game more easily. A dog's nose defines his world as he sniffs his way around the different odours that most humans don't notice. Humans have 5 million scent detectors but dogs have nearly 300 million and they can tell which way the wind is blowing and exactly where the smell is coming from by sniffing the air, pointing their wet muzzle moistened by tear ducts which run all the way down the nose and dissolve scent molecules for identification by receptor cells.

The relationship between man and dog is unique and special. Dogs will bark furiously, alerting all around to approaching danger. They 'get wind' of danger minutes before humans do even if the danger does not directly concern them and bark. This early warning system has saved many a life. One morning I was walking back from the beach and over the grass close to where Blue was tied up. He began to bark like mad in a very urgent fashion and perhaps telepathically communicated a sense of danger to me because I looked down at my feet and there was a very dangerous thick, long snake scuttling across the grass. The snake was shocked by my presence and headed for cover but within a few minutes it went on the attack so I scooped Blue up in my arms and we closed ourselves inside the house. The snake went around and around the house, desperately looking for an entrance, for 45 minutes before it gave up and slithered away.

Blue can tell when someone was going to approach our front door well before the person has even turned into the driveway – can Blue read minds and understand intention? Or is it due to his incredible hearing? Dogs can hear a greater frequency of sounds than we can and before domestication they used this to trap prey and escape predators. A dog can hear a sound 600 feet away but we are limited to about 60 feet. They have 18 separate muscles which enable them to move their ears towards the sound to pinpoint the direction of the sound.

Like most dogs, Blue knows what we want and even cocks his head to one side when we talk to him as if he understands every word. It is like living with someone who is deaf and dumb. He can anticipate what happens next and even how we are feeling. Maybe his extraordinary smelling powers extend to smelling the pheromones that we give off and that is how he reads our moods. He understands our emotional states better than many humans, perhaps due to body language and the smells we give off. When an argument breaks out between myself and Ivan, Blue runs for cover either outside in the garden or under the bed.

He has plenty of adventure in his life. Ivan invites him often to swim with him but he is not keen on waves. Blue tends to cling to Ivan in the water and the only time he is keen to swim is back to the shore to end the excursion where he sits patiently on the beach, waiting for Ivan to come out of the water. He has also been out on a water-ski where he can observe turtles at close range. Being on a boat is not exactly his idea of a good time but he goes along with it –

well, what else can he do?

His favourite sports involve running. He sometimes is taken to visit a neighbor's dog who lives on acreage and Blue loves to tear around the place, jumping into the dam and racing around their mobile home as if he owns it. He is not above stealing the food from his host dog who is much slower than Blue and just looks confused when Blue runs circles around him.

Blue is very smart and knows when to keep a low profile and the differences between Ivan and myself. Ivan insists that Blue should live outside whilst I like to have his company, especially when Ivan stays in the other house and I am alone. There has been the odd occasion when Blue has been frightened by the sound of a big branch falling off a palm tree and he has scratched the door in fright, demanding admittance. Or else there is a snake wandering around. This could happen in the middle of the night and I get up and let Blue into the house, whispering to him to lie down and stay where he is. At first, he would follow me to my room, his name tag jingling on his collar, and find himself ejected by Ivan. Over time he has learnt to keep quiet and keep still.

Ivan also bans Blue from sitting near the dining table when we are eating and Blue is clever enough to remove himself entirely. However, when I am sitting alone, he sits next to me with a look that would melt snow. How can I resist? Most times I allow him to lick my plate at the end of the meal, rather like allowing a kid to lick the bowl after a cake has been mixed.

Blue is very much like a small child and suffers from separation anxiety like a lot of small children but I find this is quickly relieved by the sight of a dog biscuit or bone. Fortunately we can leave Blue alone for a few hours and have a bit of freedom to go to see a movie or a show, something that is impossible to do with a child.

For the first few years when Blue was left alone, he would escape from the back garden. It didn't seem to matter how much time we had spent blocking up gaps and holes, he always found a way out, including digging under fences and gates. We often had phone calls from neighbors giving us the location of the dog but by the time we got there, he would have disappeared. With age, this problem is resolving itself but whenever we feel that he may disappear, we tie him up and leave him with a big bone. When he is being tied up, he knows what is coming and his tail begins to wag uncontrollably, his eyes grow big and he salivates.

One night Blue ran away whilst we were out at a restaurant. We searched everywhere for him with a strong light but to no avail. We were worried about dingoes but eventually had to leave him to his fate. I got up in the middle of the night and gazed at the street, wondering where he could be and praying that he was safe. I could hear snoring coming from the side of the house and there, behind the gate that I had left open, was Blue. He had come home but didn't dare go to sleep in his kennel because he knew that he had done something wrong.

When Blue turns his beautiful orange eyes onto us, or cuddles into us, we feel as if we have won Lotto. He keeps me fit, walking him twice a day. He shows me what real love is by staying close by me most of the time and showing me so much love. Through Blue I have learnt to let life happen and not worry about it. He just lives on a day to day basis and is fed and well cared for. He never argues or raises his voice. He is not prone to offering unwanted opinions. He hates arguments and runs into the garden whenever Ivan and I have words. He rejoices when he sees Ivan and I hugging each other and tries to join in.

I have never had a child but through Blue, I understand how we end up completely besotted by something that we are responsible for. He is the epitome of unconditional love which makes me feel like a millionaire.

BLUE, THE FATHER

I always wondered what Blue looked like as a puppy and how he would have acted. Blue came into our lives at 12 months. To train a dog he must be at least 6 months old and the training takes 6 months. He would steal something such as a shoe or a sock and run outside with it to chew on it. I know that babies love to chew on things, which is why we give them a teething ring. Chewing helps their teeth to develop normally.

A neighbor with a pure bred beagle was very keen to have Blue father some puppies. He had six boys, unfortunately one of them died. It is believed that he got stuck in the birth canal which necessitated a Caeserian section and he survived just 24 hours. We buried him on the beach.

I visited the five puppies regularly. For the first week they were tiny beings with closed eyes and velvet ears which apparently could not hear. All they wanted was to suckle. They rapidly grew and so did their teeth. One in particular, Maverick, was a real biter. Ivan was offered money or a puppy and he took the latter because he fell in love with a puppy that had an arrow marking on his head, hence the name Arrow.

The puppies were so beautiful that people were offering to buy them and the local butcher even said 'name your price' when the bitch's owner took one of the puppies into his shop.

Ivan is a collector as anyone who has visited his house can tell you, so he found it very difficult to give up the puppy that he had named. Of course, as soon as he named the puppy I knew there was going to be great difficulty in selling him to someone. Ivan came up with all sorts of excuses to keep him but at the same time, he let me walk him twice a day, along with Blue, feed him and generally take care of him.

Originally I told Ivan that the puppy was not going to come into the house until he was sold. He was offered a thousand dollars for the beautiful puppy but instead sold him to a friend in Melbourne – a 3 hour flight away from us in the Whitsundays in Queensland – for half that. That in itself was a saga as the friend said he was selling his house and could not take him immediately. He sent the cheque which I immediately banked and then the excuses started on his side.

Meantime, Arrow did keep me entertained up to a point. Blue proved to be a very indulgent father. Arrow followed him everywhere like a shadow. I believe Blue knew that he was family because early on I saw Arrow take a bone out of Blue's mouth without any problems and Blue would cede his place on the bed or cushion to Arrow when he tried snuggling up to him. I think he just wanted some peace and quiet.

I know I did.

During the first week that he came to us, Ivan took him to his house on the beach and as he was so small and new, he did not need to be on a lead, shadowing Blue every inch of the way – this only lasted until he was about 14 weeks old and then he wanted to branch out on his own.

The first time we walked them together and Blue did a poo on the beach, Arrow examined his father's behind very carefully and got covered with excreta which Ivan had to wash off in the sea. Arrow also enjoyed taking his father for a walk i.e. hanging onto the lead. When he first lost his footing he got dragged along the beach in the sand, front paws tucked under him. He loved this and did this when walking on grass too. I thought his little red belly was due to his diet until one day it dawned on me that it came from his being dragged along.

Arrow was incredibly cheeky whilst Blue is subdued. I put this down to the fact that Blue was living tied up in someone's backyard as a puppy, then at 6 months he went into training. It was probably tough for a little dog. Arrow left his mother but immediately

found his father. They play together a lot, usually chasing and biting one another's head, face and legs. Arrow often ends up on his back begging for mercy which he immediately gets but within seconds he is on the attack once again.

Arrow gained confidence every day. He liked to lie on the settee rather than the floor and as I knew that he would be leaving me, I did not try to correct him. I liked to see him making himself comfortable! But if he overstepped the mark and I tried to make him jump down, he would bite, bark and snarl.

He also had no qualms about jumping on the coffee table and even tried lapping my glass of wine when my back was turned! I had to be very tidy because if I didn't put things away, they would get dragged out into the garden to be chewed – shoes, clothes, television remote controls et al. Clothes worn below the knees were a big distraction and open to be ripped up.

Walks were not too difficult as he is like Blue's shadow but with time he got a lot of confidence and ran off only to be dragged back and put on the lead. Have you tried to walk two active dogs on separate leads? I don't recommend it. You end up with your arms being pulled behind your back sometimes.

Arrow would get under the bed and chew on the leg of the bed, or the drawer handle or the corner of the table or the settee. Everything bears the prints of his passage.

ARROW THE SON

"Look at me, look what I have got" Arrow seemed to beg as he flew past with a shoe, doll, toy, pen or whatever in his mouth. He begged to be noticed and chased. He wanted interaction of any sort. In quiet moments he would sit at my feet or when hanging out the washing he lay on the ground close by. Of course, he had the odd nip at clothes that were being hung out to dry. Washing day was a trial because anything in the basket on the ground was fair game and anything hanging above his head could be torn from the line and used as a toy.

He was a playful soul, full of energy and always trying to get either myself or Blue to chase him. Blue would usually come good late afternoon in the cool of the day and then he launched himself into full scale play with his son – he bit his head, legs, paws. Arrow bit his father's ears, or legs. He licked any wounds and even licked his private parts. Blue seemed to know just how far he could go without hurting him although from time to time there was the odd yelp escaping from Arrow. They loved to get each other in a headlock, rather more difficult for Arrow who had a smaller mouth.

As he grew, Arrow became a handful. He loved to sit with me on the settee except of course this was not allowed (when Ivan is around) but when I tried to get him off, he got really mad, snarling and trying to bite me. My hands and arms were full of scratches and bites where I came off second best.

When I realized that Arrow was psycho I felt a bit of a pang – at least he was only a dog not a human child and on top of that, one that had already been sold to someone else –but still. A bit of a failure to realize that you are raising a psychotic dog. One day I tried to get him off the settee and he went completely psycho, jumping, biting, scratching, anything to stay where he is. Only by throwing him to his father outside was I able to stop the rot.

When he sat on the sofa he lay back on the cushions as if that is where he was meant to be. Completely at home whilst his father would lie on the floor. I gave him a little cloth to lie on but there was hell to pay if he went to lie somewhere else – especially when he did a little pee on a suede settee. Trying to get him off put me in danger of being bitten but one thing I noticed is that when I started screaming, Blue took off. He always avoids confrontation and hates arguments. Even when Ivan and I argue he quietly runs out into the garden and sometimes hides under the bushes.

My parents told me they had my sister to keep me company – they used to watch me outside in the garden all alone, sometimes looking through the hedge at the neighbour's children, playing together. How many people have two dogs so they keep each other company when the owner is at work. One thing is for sure, Arrow would have been a real handful if not for Blue. Blue provided an endless source of entertainment for Arrow who would nibble his ears, bite his paws, ride around on his back and hang around his neck.

When walking them, Arrow would hang on to Blue's lead and we dragged him along the ground between us. It was alright til he got to four months of age and heavier.

In the very hot part of the summer, the dogs would have an early morning walk and I do mean early – just after dawn because they wouldn't leave me alone. When I fed Arrow his meal, I had to give Blue something so that he didn't feel left out. They would then lie down somewhere with a breeze and wait for the heat to pass. They reminded me so much of small children who required a mid morning and mid afternoon nap.

They often looked at me as if I was going to provide some entertainment and when this did not eventuate, they would race around and around the garden, fighting, tearing things up between them and generally having a good time.

Arrow had something in common with small children – he put everything into his mouth. I guess not having hands this was the only thing he could do. His teeth were sharp like razors but he did try to control his biting when taking small amounts of food from my fingers.

Having a second dog made me realize that dogs really do have personalities – Blue is a very quiet, well-behaved dog. Like a lot of dogs he is very afraid of thunderstorms and lies trembling under Ivan's bed. As a child with my sister, we would both run and hide behind Dad's chair during storms, even when Dad wasn't home.

Blue is timid but crafty and has often run out of the house whilst I was bending down getting washing out of the machine – I would call and realize that he had made an escape.

Arrow on the other hand was fearless. When I saw him lying back on the settee I tried to coax him off it by offering a small biscuit whereas Ivan just gives him a big swipe. Arrow didn't care and as soon as Ivan left, he was back on the settee, leaning back on the cushions like a pasha whilst Blue just watched him from his position on the floor.

One night we had a terrible storm and Blue cowered behind Ivan's bed. Arrow had fallen asleep but woke up an hour or so later wondering where Blue had got to. He began to whimper but Ivan kept an eye on him and he went back to sleep – his first night alone in his life with thunder and lightening crashing all around him most of the night. Arrow seemed fearless.

When we are small we all need quite a bit of sleep and when we grow old we tire easily and dogs are the same. Blue is getting quieter as he ages – thank goodness.

Just like children, a routine is very important. Dogs need to know that they are going to be walked twice a day and fed and usually get edgy when things don't happen on time, same time every day. It is almost as if they are wearing a watch. When tired, they get grizzly and difficult to handle and need to be put down for a rest. They do say that children need routine so that they don't stress.

Arrow looks more like his mother than his father – with her long black eyelashes. He appears to be growing into his big paws and very long ears. When the puppies first came into the world they were all black and white, like little jersey cows and the colour tan started to appear within a few weeks. Some have more than others and one looks exactly like his father with a very tan head.

Blue is a very attractive dog with a lot of white on belly and legs and the white streak up the middle of the head as they all do as well as white tip on the tail.

That has been bred into them so that when they run through long grass after the prey, they can be seen – rather like cars driving through the bush with flags on the antenna.

Arrow started off with beautiful tan ears on the inside which gradually started to cover the top of his head. His face is tan with a lot of black rather like a bandit's mask – very appropriate in his case as he is always stealing.

He jumps on tables and takes whatever he can find and is not above trying to steal food.

He is much loved by his new family in Melbourne who seem to be able to handle him – he has the best of everything and lives with another beagle called Toby.

Blue was very good with his son and gave him everything. We believe that Blue knows that Arrow is his own flesh and blood as he has even let him take a bone out of his mouth and Blue really loves his food. He really looked after him, giving up his bed. Arrow lay so close to Blue that Blue would get up and give him his spot which Arrow was only too happy to take – he was very spoiled by all of us. How is he going to turn out – anyone's guess but he seems to be doing OK. When I yelled at Arrow, Blue rushed out as much to say "It wasn't me".

Everyone says that children appear to have more fun playing with the packaging than the expensive presents on Christmas day – well, it is the same with dogs. Empty packages, empty plastic bottles (with a few dog biscuits inside, like a rattle), rags, old shoes. Unfortunately it is difficult for dogs to tell the difference between permitted toys and shoes that we are still wearing. So when Arrow grabbed something – clothes, shoes, television remote control – and I wrestled with him to get it back, he thought it was a big game and would not let go.

I do know of a baby that often bit his mother, until he went to school in fact, and my arms and legs are full of bites and scratches. Dogs have sharp nails and teeth and when they play together, they don't mind using them on each other.

BLUE THE TEACHER

A parent is meant to teach its offspring how to live in the world. My job was to teach Arrow the puppy not to sit on the furniture, lie on the beds, steal food and run off.

Blue taught his son to eat grass to keep his intestines in good working order and how to follow a scent.

Blue would set off in the lead, pointing out interesting areas by sniffing. Arrow followed suit but I could see that he was not sure what they were sniffing as he looked sideways at his Dad from time to time. Blue is always on a lead nowadays as he is an escape artist par excellence. Arrow was happy to trot along by his Dad but if there was any food on the path, especially from my German friend, Ilse who regularly feeds all the dogs and birds that pass in front of her house, Arrow became hard to control and I had to put him on a lead to drag him away from her house or put him on a lead so that he did not take off back to her house at the end of the walk.

Blue played a lot and sometimes it looked as if it was Arrow teaching the father how to play again as Blue was an old father at 8. It was wonderful to see the whole family together – Mom, Dad and five sons. The children raced each other down the beach whilst the parents brought up the rear on their respective leads.

Lightening certainly takes after his mother and is quiet and sedate but Arrow was getting more and more like his father. This could only mean trouble.

Arrow was very naughty – the only way to describe it. It was all a game but it got quite out of hand. I realize that to him I was a playmate whilst Ivan was the authority figure and this is very much in evidence when Arrow forgot himself and started throwing himself at me, with teeth and nails in order to win the game.

"Ivan, help" I shouted and Ivan walked in with arms folded and just glared at him. Meanwhile Arrow retreated to a neutral position with an angelic look on his face – 'It wasn't me, Dad". I could not bear it when Ivan felt the need to hit Arrow but as he said it was just reinforcing the point. Arrow didn't seem to mind at all and just bounced right back.

In fact, I looked at this new little puppy and wondered if that is how we are all born – full of self confidence and when we get a bit beaten, we can bounce back. Are some children beaten so hard in childhood that it is just not possible to bounce back from such a beating? Does it happen so often that the child feels totally unloved and useless? Ivan slapped Arrow and I kissed him. Talk about mixed messages but is this why he just bounced back?

CONCLUSION

Never having wanted to have children, I find the constant need for attention a bit of a pain. But who can resist a cry from a tiny creature that needs you? Dogs seem to have developed many different cries and yelps – the rough barking signals danger and I have heard it when walking across the lawn which stopped me putting my foot on a very dangerous snake that then bailed us up inside the house for 45 minutes, Blue barking all the time. The big, frank bark to let you know that someone has come to the door and could be dangerous. The excited welcome yelps of welcome when that person is recognized as a friend.

Then there is the tiny little call for attention – only my attention. Let us not let the alpha male, Ivan, know that I am back after running away earlier in the day. Just open the door and let me in quietly so that I can sleep somewhere safe. The whiney bark calling for

food. The tiny yelp to show me that the water bowl is empty.

Dogs certainly have no problems communicating – often an intense look. Blue would come into my room in the morning and look intensely at me. If I ignored him, he went away but when he was fed up he would come and put his front paws on the bed to wake me. He would sit outside patiently waiting to be taken for a walk. You could not ignore him. At mealtimes he would walk around the table, not close enough to be shouted at, not in a manner that could be interpreted as begging for which he would get a slap but in the manner of saying 'Hey don't forget me'.

Blue rules the roost. Mostly he sleeps indoors, unbeknown to Ivan. In fact, Blue sleeps under his bed most of the time. He has been thrown out in the wee small hours of the morning when Ivan has got up and found him or he starts having nightmares and making shrill barking noises. I am his slave. But is that not the lot of many mothers with their children?

I will not be unhappy when Blue eventually comes to the end of his life. It will give me back my freedom and I will be able to go on long walks without any fear. I have put off a few trips because of Blue.

Beagles usually live 12-14 years and Blue will be 10 in a few months. He sleeps more but it is very hot here. Ivan and I have rarely left him alone. We have been very good to Blue, making sure that he has everything he wants and especially providing company. He is usually not left alone for more than half a day and even then, he gets a big bone to keep him busy.

We have met our obligations. Pity I cannot say

the same for everyone else. Abandoned pets and even abandoned or badly treated children. Anyone thinking of having a child would be wise to have a dog first and see how they handle that first.

Blue has provided endless hours of amusement. It is interesting to see the world through his eyes. He has been my one and only dog. As I am now 68 I don't see myself replacing him when he goes to doggy heaven.

Dog owners all have wonderful stories. Many, like me, believe that dogs are psychic. When Blue stares intently at me, I often ask him what he wants and then the idea comes into my head – not too difficult to guess as it concerns food or a walk. Dogs are wonderful company – non-judgmental, always ready to listen, they don't make stupid comments, they don't chatter endlessly about nothing and they put their head on your feet and gaze lovingly at you. Even when reprimanded it only takes minutes before all is forgiven. These are the things to live on when they have gone. Salutations to all other dog owners who love their pets.

THE END

Printed in Great Britain
by Amazon